Loon Summer

FIELD NOTES

Loon Summer

An amazing and true account of loon parenting
for adults and children to share

BY SANDY GILLUM

PHOTOGRAPHY BY
WOODY HAGGE
LEN BACKUS
DOUG KILLIAN
DAVID RIPPON
SANDY GILLUM
JEFF RICHTER

FIELD NOTES PRESS
EAGLE RIVER, WISCONSIN

© Len Backus

Published by Field Notes Press
PO Box 2437
Eagle River, WI 54521
Email: fieldnotes@nnex.net

ISBN: 978-0-9801201-0-3

Library of Congress Control Number:
2008920020

Designed by Patricia Bickner
www.anewleaf-books.com

Printed in Canada

© Woody Hagge

To all those wonder filled by our natural world,
especially Don, Jane, Ellie, and Katie

—S.S.G.

With special thanks to
Mike,
Jayne and Rollie,
Christi and Dick,
Bernie,
and Jane N.

AUTHOR'S NOTE

Common loons are called northern divers in some parts of the world and indeed these birds are! Using their powerful legs and webbed feet, they dive for food with striking underwater speed and agility. In the watery depths of northern lakes, they catch minnows, small fish, aquatic insects like dragonfly larva, and sometimes even crayfish for food. In the air, the flight of these solid-boned birds is driven by forceful wing power. Walking on land is quite another thing. Loons have short legs set well to the rear of their bodies and they have large webbed feet. The design of their bodies makes walking on land labored and as clumsy as penguins waddling. Loons usually limit their attempts at walking to only when they climb out of the water onto their nests to incubate their eggs. Most of their lifetimes are spent on water, unless they are flying.

GLOSSARY

habitat   A place in nature where a particular animal can find its natural food, shelter, and a safe place to raise its young.

incubate   To warm eggs with body heat under the breast or wing of a bird.

migration   The seasonal movement of birds and animals in response to weather and the availability of food and water.

molt   To shed feathers and grow new feathers in their place.

rogue   A loon that does not have a territory or mate and roams from lake to lake to feed. Rogues sometimes attempt to drive off one loon of a territorial pair and then take over that territory and the remaining mate.

territorial lake A lake defended by a pair of loons as the lake where they spend the summer breeding season and raise their chicks.

territorial pair A male and female loon who defend a lake from intruding loons and who, if everything is in their favor, will raise chicks there.

*Here is a true account
of one loon family's
amazing summer . . .*

*S*pring was coming. At noon the sun was higher, and with each passing day it set farther north in the western sky.

A particular Common Loon had spent the winter fishing in the warm waters of the Gulf of Mexico, west of Key West, near the Dry Tortugas Islands. Over the last several weeks, Loon had molted his gray and dusky winter feathers and in their place had grown the handsome new black and white feathers of his summer plumage. When he was a chick, his eyes were brown, but now as an adult loon he had piercing, red-colored eyes.

It was April. The time to migrate had come. Loon left the warm tropical waters of the gulf, and day by day, night by night, he flew north. There were familiar stars and lakes and rivers to guide him. He had migrated south along this route in the fall of his first year. He had lived on the ocean until he was three years old. In the spring of his third year, he made his first flight north from the gulf, following this same familiar route.

Loon flew farther north. He took advantage of rivers and lakes to rest and feed on fish. As he neared the Great Lakes, he turned northwest and flew over Lake Michigan. He began to fly above familiar rivers in Wisconsin that pointed him toward Owl Lake. Owl Lake was near Blue Lake . . . the lake where he had hatched eight years ago. His parents still returned to Blue Lake and each summer they raised one or two loon chicks there. So Loon was not welcome on the lake where he hatched, because his parents still defended it as their territory.

He had found no loons on nearby Owl Lake. This little lake had plenty of fish and he now defended it as his very own territory. Each spring since he was four years old, he returned. Somehow, he remembered Owl Lake, perhaps by its shape or its position among other lakes or maybe its distance from the river. Just how he remembered the little lake is a mystery known only to him.

As Loon winged over the northern rivers, ice was breaking up. Each day he flew farther north and found stretches of rivers where there was just enough open water to land and to dive for fish. He flew on and on until he reached open water on the Wisconsin River near Owl Lake . . . the lake that would be the summer home for him and his mate and where they would raise their chicks.

Each day, Loon took off from the river and flew over Owl Lake. Each day he circled it. Day by day, the ice there grew darker and darker, and more and more cracks appeared. Sometimes the melting ice even made groaning and booming sounds. One breezy morning, the sky was a clear deep blue and the spring sun warmed Loon's black back. After fishing on the river, he flew to Owl Lake and could see that the ice was melting fast and there was open water just wide enough and long enough for a loon to land. He glided in and slid across the water. Landing! Summer home!

Owl Lake was excellent loon habitat. Not only was the lake large enough for loon landings and take-offs, it had a supply of fish and minnows enough for a whole loon family, several sites along the shore suitable for a loon to build a nest and only a few homes that were set back in the woods from the shore. The people that lived there enjoyed mostly quiet-water activities and watching birds.

In a few days, Loon's mate would return to the clear waters of Owl Lake. While waiting for her, Loon spent hours fishing . . . catching and eating bluegills and perch. He approached and circled other loons that landed on his lake. He penguin-danced on top of the water, chasing them all away, because none of them was his mate. He even called loud tremolos and yodels to announce his "ownership" of this lake to any loon flying overhead. Only male loons can yodel those eerie up and down notes and they do so to announce to other loons that their lake is occupied by a territorial pair of loons and other loons are not welcome. Both male and female loons can make the three-noted tremolo calls and they use this call when they become alarmed.

© Woody Hagge

Three days passed. Then out of the morning sky glided another loon, who looked exactly like all other common loons. This new arrival circled, landed on the water, and paddled with its large webbed feet across Owl Lake toward Loon. He did not yodel or tremolo. He hooted. She hooted softly back. As they approached each other, both loons nodded their heads and dipped their bills, and somehow . . . just somehow, they recognized each other. They swam side-by-side and then dived for food together. Why they chose each other as mates is another mystery known only to them, but this spring they had both returned to Owl Lake again, where they would build their nest, mate, and raise chicks. These loons had built nests on the shore in past summers and each year the female had laid two eggs, but the eggs had been stolen twice—eaten one year by a raccoon and the following summer a fox had raided the nest.

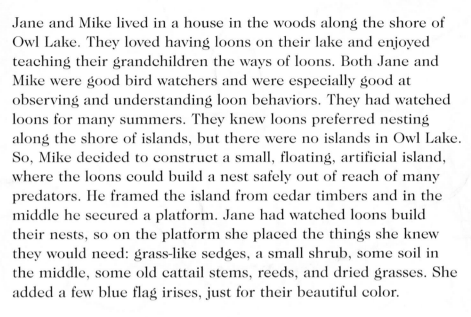

Jane and Mike lived in a house in the woods along the shore of Owl Lake. They loved having loons on their lake and enjoyed teaching their grandchildren the ways of loons. Both Jane and Mike were good bird watchers and were especially good at observing and understanding loon behaviors. They had watched loons for many summers. They knew loons preferred nesting along the shore of islands, but there were no islands in Owl Lake. So, Mike decided to construct a small, floating, artificial island, where the loons could build a nest safely out of reach of many predators. He framed the island from cedar timbers and in the middle he secured a platform. Jane had watched loons build their nests, so on the platform she placed the things she knew they would need: grass-like sedges, a small shrub, some soil in the middle, some old cattail stems, reeds, and dried grasses. She added a few blue flag irises, just for their beautiful color.

Bald eagles will eat loon eggs. Knowing this, Mike strung ropes between two vertical sticks along two sides of the "island." Eagles glide in on outstretched wings when they land; the ropes would keep bald eagles from having enough clearance for landing. Mike anchored the little island in the lake far enough away from shore so that heron, mink, raccoons, or foxes would not easily find and eat the loons' eggs. Even though it had taken a summer or two, Mike and Jane were pleased when the loon pair figured out that the island was a safe place for them to build their nest. The little island was really perfect: anchored in a cove, sheltered from the prevailing northwest winds, and the materials they needed to build their flat, dish-shaped nest were already there!

Loon and his mate fished and ate and fished and ate, but when the end of May neared, they climbed onto the "island" and began to arrange their shallow nest. A week later the female loon laid one large greenish-brown egg, with some dark brown spots. The first egg was followed by a second egg the next day. Mother Loon tucked the eggs under her breast and wings to keep them warm. Father Loon helped incubate the eggs, too. The loon parents took turns—Father Loon would sit on the eggs for about two hours and then Mother Loon would incubate the eggs for several hours. After their turn incubating the eggs, each adult loon would swim off to feed on fish. Before sitting down to incubate the eggs, the parent would roll each egg over to keep the developing chick embryo from sticking to the inside of its shell.

The loon sitting on the eggs would watch the sky and lake for trouble. If it saw a bald eagle or a loon flying overhead, it would tremolo an alarm to its mate. If it was Father Loon that spotted the danger, he might yodel loudly. The loon who was not sitting on the eggs spent most of its time diving and eating fish. After feeding, each loon would preen its feathers by cleaning, oiling, and straightening them, one by one. Mother and Father Loon shared caring for their eggs for almost a month.

© Woody Hagge

Twenty-eight days passed.

It was almost July when one egg began pipping. Using the egg tooth on the end of its bill, the little chick chipped and cracked its way out of its egg. Both Father and Mother Loon listened and watched. The whole time the chick was hatching, Mother Loon kept it and the other egg warm. In a few hours the first chick tumbled free of its shell. It did not look much like a loon. Its black down was wet and pasted to its body. It lurched around the nest, sometimes ducking under the wing of Mother Loon; sometimes tumbling out into the sun. All the while the first chick was hatching and drying, Father Loon circled the "island" nest, looking and listening and waiting, sometimes making "mewing" calls to Mother Loon and the new chick.

Several hours later, the first chick's feathers had dried and it became a fluffy little ball of black with shining brown eyes. It scrambled hungrily about the nest. Father Loon softly hooted to the chick as he brought a bluegill to the edge of the nest, then a perch, then a large minnow. The chick refused all these fish. They were just too big! Next, Father Loon brought an aquatic invertebrate—a small water insect called a dragonfly nymph. Just right! The chick quickly swallowed this little insect—and Father Loon brought more. After several meals, the chick followed the hoots of Father Loon and launched on its first swim. The chick naturally floated and bobbed about on top of the water. But it soon got tired and cold. The chick scrambled back up the side of the "island" into the nest, and hid under the warm wing of Mother Loon. The next day, the second chick hatched, dried, scrambled about, and took its first swim. Within hours, the whole loon family swam away from the island nest for the last time, never to return this year. The parent loons paddled with the chicks to a quiet bay across the lake. This "nursery bay" had food for the chicks—aquatic insects, small minnows, and even some newly hatched fish fry.

Mother and Father Loon fed the chicks often, and by the end of a week the chicks had grown large enough to eat a few minnows that their parents brought them. They ate the minnows head-first, because they slip down easier that way. The chicks begged for food often and grew visibly day by day. Father and Mother Loon began taking turns caring for the chicks. One parent always stayed with the chicks, while the other parent dove all across Owl Lake catching fish for itself.

The little chicks got tired and chilled sometimes. To get warm or to nap, one or both of the chicks would climb up onto the back of one of their parents and snuggle down in the warm black feathers. At other times, one would simply tuck its little head under the wing of one of the adults and float and doze in the darkness. Sometimes one of the adult loons took a nap, too, by tucking its beak under one of its wings and closing its eyes.

© Woody Hagge

Father and Mother Loon were very careful to preen their beautiful black and white feathers. The chicks watched their parents care for each feather. In about eight weeks the chicks would have big feathers, too. The chicks would fledge, losing their downy feathers. In their place would grow new, adult-sized, gray feathers with creamy-colored spots.

Days passed. One starry night, when the chicks were several weeks old, biologists came to Owl Lake and carefully caught the loon family. Each bird was gently weighed and colored bands were put on their legs: a silver and a colored band on one leg and two colored bands on the other leg. The biologists had put leg bands on Mother and Father Loon several years ago, so this year they just checked the weight and health of both adults. Every banded loon has a color band combination that no other loon has. The brightly colored bands come in red, yellow, white, orange, blue, or green, plus a unique numbered aluminum band. Leg bands do not harm or bother loons and the colors of the bands allow biologists to identify each bird at a distance, using binoculars or a telescope.

© Woody Hagge

A week after the chicks were banded, Jane and Mike noticed that Father Loon was yodeling more and more often at loons flying over Owl Lake. Some of these loons landed on the lake. Mother Loon would tremolo an alarm too. Sometimes a "stranger" loon—a rogue loon, apparently without a territory or mate of its own—would land on the lake and swim toward the loon family, threatening both parents and their chicks. The survival of the chicks depended on the parent loons being able to drive the rogue loon away, because rogue loons often kill chicks and drive off one of the territorial loons in an attempt to gain the territory and a mate.

When a rogue loon landed, the parent loons gave hoots to the chicks, which signaled the chicks to duck into the reeds and hide from the intruder.

©Woody Hagge

Once the chicks were safely hidden, Father and Mother Loon would swim towards the rogue loon. They would tuck their chins like a pelican and jerk their heads deliberately in and out of the water in an attempt to frighten the intruding loon away. If that gesture were not enough, the parent loons would penguin dance on top of the water in an effort to make themselves look big and menacing. Often they would dive and chase the rogue underwater and sometimes try to stab it with their sharp, pointed beaks. Jane and Mike observed more and more often the parent loons having to stop their usual pattern of feeding and caring for their chicks and chase off an intruding loon. Often they would chase the rogue across the water, or if it dove, swim after it underwater.

Owl Lake, where this loon family nested, was very near two other small lakes, each about a quarter of a mile from the other, as a loon would fly. Father and Mother Loon seemed to include both Key and Scot lakes as part of their feeding territory. While one parent tended the chicks, the other adult would often fly to either Scot or Key Lake and spend time there diving for fish. After an hour or so, that parent would always fly back to Owl Lake, skim to a landing, preen its feathers, and exchange chick-tending time with its mate.

As rogue loons landed on Owl Lake more often, the pattern of the parents tending and feeding the chicks and then feeding and preening themselves was becoming a challenge. One day, Jane could not find Father or Mother Loon or either of their chicks on Owl Lake. For two days, Jane looked for them with her binoculars. She even kayaked along the entire shore. The loon family was missing! Jane called her friend Kay, a biologist who studied loons and who had studied this particular loon pair for years. Kay wondered whether the chicks had been killed and the adults had flown to either Scot or Key Lake. Jane and Kay agreed to meet at the edge of the forest near Scot Lake. Kay brought a telescope and Jane brought her binoculars.

The two friends hiked through red pines and a sugar maple forest to the edge of Scot Lake. Jane spotted an adult loon floating on the lake near the far shore. Kay focused on the adult with her scope. It had leg bands! It was Mother Loon! And swimming beside it was a banded chick! They were the loons from Jane's lake—Owl Lake! *But the chicks could not fly yet!*

AMAZING! Mother Loon and the chick had to have waddled up the steep bank along Owl Lake's shore, through the thick woods strewn with stumps and logs, around shrubs, across a country road, then down through a wide ditch and somehow up a steep, rocky embankment to the edge of a large and high meadow. The beautiful meadow crowned the highest point in the county and was covered with tall grasses, daisies, orange hawkweeds, and black-eyed Susans. After finding their way across the top of the meadow and without being tall enough to see Scot Lake through the wildflowers and grasses, Mother Loon and her chick must have continued down to where the meadow met another woods. These woods were strewn with large boulders that must have seemed like mountains to the loons, but after winding their way though them, they would have arrived on the shore of little Scot Lake. This was *more* than a quarter of a mile and Mother Loon and her chick had walked it!

But where were Father Loon and the second chick? Jane and Kay went back to Owl Lake and hunted the shoreline and the surface of the lake with binoculars, but they could not find even one loon.

Another dark night passed. Morning came and Jane still could not find any loons on Owl Lake. She hiked to Scot Lake where she and Kay had seen Mother Loon and the banded chick the day before. She hiked up through the tangled woods, down through the ditch, up over the meadow hill through the waist-high grasses and wildflowers, past the fox den . . . where no one seemed to be at home . . . around the boulders strewn in the woods at the meadow's edge and on though the woods to the shore. With her binoculars, Jane saw *two* adult loons *and* two loon chicks in Scot Lake! All were fishing and feeding just as normal loons do.

Jane rushed home to call Kay. She asked Kay to bring her telescope and check the color bands on all the loons at Scot Lake. Kay arrived shortly. The two friends talked excitedly. They hiked to the shore and set up Kay's scope. WOW! It was the whole loon family from Owl Lake! All the loons had waddled to Scot Lake! What a very long, long distance and what rough terrain for loons to walk! Kay and Jane realized what an amazing struggle Father and Mother Loon had gone through to protect their chicks!

The loon family spent the remainder of the summer peacefully on Scot Lake. The chicks grew larger, learned to dive for food, and fledged, growing adult-sized feathers. Once the chicks had big feathers, Mother and Father Loon taught them how to fly. In September, Father and Mother Loon left on their migration south, flying toward the Gulf of Mexico . . . toward the waters at the tip of Florida and westward toward the ocean that surrounds the Dry Tortugas Islands.

The chicks remained on Scot Lake almost a month longer, feeding and practicing take-offs, flying and landing. They were last seen in late October, just before a fall snow shower. They flew south, probably following the same route their parents had flown. How the chicks knew this route is a wonderful mystery, but from generation to generation loon chicks fly to the warm waters of the ocean starting with their first migration. There, on the ocean, in waters rich with fish, these loon chicks will live until they are three or four years old. Then they will molt, growing beautiful black feathers with white spots and neck stripes, and their eyes will turn from brown to red. When their first migration spring comes, they will fly north to find their own territorial lake, to find a mate and raise chicks of their own.

These chicks surely had amazing parents!

It was an awesome loon summer!

WHAT YOU CAN DO TO CONSERVE COMMON LOON HABITAT

Long ago, people told stories about their experiences with loons. Today, these legends remind us of the long-standing relationship between loons and humans. Many lake residents and visitors throughout the common loon's northern breeding grounds take an active role in loon conservation. You can be a part of this legacy by getting involved with citizen monitoring through your local loon preservation group, and by giving presentations to your lake association or community on loon-related issues, such as the dangers of lead in fishing tackle, restoring shoreline for nesting sites, and maintaining a no-wake zone around established nests and young chicks. Understanding the needs of loons will help you help them. For more information, visit the LoonWatch website at www.northland.edu/loonwatch or call 715-682-1220.

Stacy Schaefer
Environmental Education Coordinator, LoonWatch Program
Sigurd Olsen Environmental Institute, Northland College, Ashland, Wisconsin